Professor Birdsong's

147 Dumbest Criminal Stories: Florida

Leonard Birdsong
Winghurst Publications

Professor Birdsong's 147 Dumbest Criminal Stories: Florida by Leonard Birdsong
© 2015 Leonard Birdsong
ISBN: 978-0-9898452-4-3

Winghurst Publications
1969 S. Alafaya Trail / Suite 303
Orlando, FL 32828-8732
www.BirdsongsLaw.com
lbirdsong@barry.edu

Disclaimer:
The facts that are recounted in the stories in this volume are true and in the public domain, as best as Professor Birdsong can determine from his research of court documents, newspapers, and wire services. The author's commentaries on these stories are his own views and opinions and do not reflect the official policy or position of any Law school, Law firm or other organization with which the author may be affiliated. The opinions provided herein are not intended to malign or defame any religion, ethnic group, club, organization, company, individual or anyone or anything. The author further covenants and represents that the work contains no matter that will incite prejudice, amount to an invasion of privacy, be libelous, obscene or otherwise unlawful or which infringe upon any proprietary interest at common law, trademark, trade secret, patent or copyright. The author is the sole proprietor of the work and all parts thereof.

Permissions:
Cover graphics: © Loopall | Dreamstime.com, © Ievgen Melamud | Dreamstime.com
Book cover design: Rik Feeney / www.RickFeeney.com

Table of Contents

Leonard Birdsong

Introduction

Professor Leonard Birdsong lives in Orlando, Florida where he teaches Criminal Law, Evidence, and Immigration Law. He has written many scholarly legal pieces since joining the legal academy.

Among his scholarly pieces are his articles entitled: *The Formation of The Caribbean Court of Justice: The Sunset of British Colonial Rule in the English Speaking Caribbean* and *The Felony Murder Doctrine Revisited: A Proposal For Calibrating Punishment that Reaffirms the Sanctity Of Human Life of Co-Felons Who Are Victims.*

This is not one of those scholarly pieces!

This volume of Professor Birdsong's 147 Dumbest Florida Criminal Stories is written just for fun and enjoyment. It showcases the many funny and weird criminal law stories from his home state of Florida.

Although he has been involved in serious criminal law work over the years as a prosecutor, a defense attorney, and a law professor, Professor Birdsong knows that it is good to get a good laugh at least once every day. That is why several years ago he began to collect and edit from the wire services and news the type of funny stories about dumb criminals that appear in this volume. This book will allow you to get a good laugh each day you read it.

Professor Birdsong thanks both his brilliant student research assistants, Megan Fletcher and Arielle Lewis, for their editorial assistance in preparation of this volume. He hopes that you will get a few good laughs from this new volume of his weird criminal law stories and his commentary accompanying each of them.

You may find other volumes of his Dumbest Criminal and Weird Criminal Law Stories at

Amazon.com or by going to his website: LeonardBirdsong.com.

Enjoy!

Leonard Birdsong

Chapter One:

Dumbest North Florida Criminals

Florida is a wonderful place to live. We have warm weather year round, lots of fun in the sun and at our beaches. Professor Birdsong loves the state! However, he has found that there are a whole host of dumb criminal law stories that come out of Florida every year. He has put a good number of them in this volume for your reading enjoyment.

These first Dumbest Florida Criminals stories are from North Florida which we, who live here, call the panhandle. The panhandle has lot of land stretching from Jacksonville in the east to Pensacola in the west. The capital city, Tallahassee, is right in the middle of the panhandle. There are many wonderful beaches along the panhandle's Gulf of Mexico coast. Enjoy these stories from North Florida.

***

It appears she was drunk and he used a driver. FORE! The father of a spring-breaker arrested for underage drinking got so angry about having to stand in a long line at the jail to pay his daughter's bail that he bashed six cars with a golf club. The irate daddy, whose 20-year-old daughter had been arrested in DeFuniak Springs, was seen on surveillance tape whacking a police car and five other vehicles in the jail parking lot, causing $1,600 in damage.

No good deed goes unpunished! Jacksonville police say Brian Jeffers stole $200 in a holdup at a sandwich shop. The shop was next door to a convenience store where Jeffers had borrowed $3 from a clerk. He was arrested when he returned to the convenience store to repay the $3 debt with the stolen money. *Idiot!*

Florida Spring breakers will soon receive beach-side service – from the police! And, it will certainly save on gas... It has been reported that police in Panama City Beach, always popular with spring breakers, have a new mobile booking unit complete with a juvenile detention area. It will be ready for the expected 250,000 to 300,000 young people expected next spring. It has been further reported that the new unit will allow police to do their work right at the beach instead of at the county jail two hours away.

He's probably on his way to Paradise Island... Authorities are searching for the former director of tourism in Okaloosa County, after he allegedly used county tax money to purchase a $710,000 yacht, and then went missing. County officials maintain they never realized he bought the boat until they received an invoice in the mail. They have no idea where he is or when he might return.

Yes, we know Faulkner wrote the novel "The Sound and the Fury" but he was not that

Faulkner....Police and workers in Salt Springs were shocked when a man plowed his 2001 Lincoln Town Car through a construction barrier, hit a worker, and barreled into a strip mall. The man turned out to be a 76-year-old man named William Faulkner. He told police he was late for a haircut.

Seems she should have been charged with assault and "bitery," instead! An allegedly intoxicated woman was so angry when her boyfriend tried to break off their relationship that she bit his leg until he bled. The 41-year-old Walton Beach woman then pointed a paintball gun at him and said, "You're not going anywhere." Police were called and proceeded to charge her with assault and battery. *Seems she should have been charged with assault and "bitery," instead!*

Things were not so "nice" in Niceville on this day. It didn't take her long to find her way back to jail. Michela Ann Jensen, 28, wound up behind bars just days after being released, when she went to a family party and began slugging her grandmother with a shoe – for selling her dog while she was locked up. And all this happened in the town of Niceville.

A squirrel hunting trip blew up in a Gainesville man's face. William Daniel Lloyd allegedly taped a live .40-caliber bullet cartridge to the end of a high powered BB gun and pulled the trigger. The pellet hit the bullet cartridge so hard, it exploded in Lloyd's face, wounding him.

Just call him Houdini! According to police, a suspected speeding motorist twice eluded police in Highland Beach, giving himself enough time to "disappear." When officers caught up with his car, which had stopped, it appeared to be empty. But as they were leaving, he took off again. They gave chase and the same thing happened. They finally realized that the suspect, who had once been arrested on a drug rap, had been quickly entering and exiting the trunk of the car via the backseat. *Ha, Ha...*

How dumb do you have to be to rob greasy spoon Waffle Houses? Marquis F, 22, wanted to pay his girlfriend's court ordered probation costs – so he allegedly robbed businesses in Pensacola to get the cash. He allegedly used a BB gun to rob a gas station and three Waffle houses, said arresting officers.

*Boy, talk about a cheapskate...*A man in Jacksonville was arrested after he walked out of a local cemetery with three bouquets of flowers he had stolen from a fresh grave. He told police that the flowers were for his girlfriend.

We wonder how the tutu went over at the jail? A macho Marine portrayed his feminine side in Gainesville by dressing up for Halloween in a tutu. On the street, he spotted a man in a wheelchair wearing an Army fatigue jacket and assumed the fellow was also in costume; offended by this, the Marine screamed at the fellow and pushed him out of the wheelchair. As it turns out, the victim was a genuine paralyzed war veteran. The Marine was quickly sent to jail for the remainder of

Halloween evening. *Again, we wonder how the tutu went over at the jail?*

*Love, love, love made her do foolish things...*A Jacksonville woman going through a bitter divorce and child custody battle was arrested for spray painting the image of broken hearts all over the sidewalks and columns of the new courthouse. Audrey Dostie, 35, also spray painted her ex-husband's corporate headquarters.

*Sounds like this guy wanted to go to jail for the free three hots and a cot...*A Fort Walton Beach man, who was allegedly trespassing in a park, told the police officer who confronted him that he wanted to urinate on the officer's patrol car – and then he did. The surprise? He was immediately arrested and taken where? *Straight to jail.*

A bit nasty wouldn't you say. Roland R, 34, of Jacksonville, has been brought up on federal charges for tampering with consumer products. What kind of products? Prosecutors maintain that their investigation revealed that

R bought, used, resealed and returned used enemas to local pharmacies that unwittingly resold them.

What a pudding head... "Hi, Mom, could you give me a ride home? I just tried to rob a liquor store" Sheriff's deputies in Okaloosa County arrested Zachariah Dalton Howard, 22, after he allegedly attempted but failed to knock off a Thumbs-Up convenience store and then telephoned his mother to pick him up, police officials say.

Chapter Two:

Dumbest Gulf Coast Florida Criminals

Professor Birdsong loves the Gulf Coast towns and its beaches. Since he has relatives in Sarasota, he travels to this part of the state often. They have some real dumb criminals over there, too. Feast your eyes on a few of them.

***

This sounds so yucky that it must be a hoax...Ugh! A report out of Tampa alleges that animal rights activists are angry over a Taco Fusion restaurant that is offering a $35 lion-meat taco. The owner claims the meat comes from big cats humanely raised on U.S. farms, but the animal activists are skeptical. The owner has gone on to contend that he will soon be offering dishes containing iguana, bear and zebra meat. *Ugh!*

It's so difficult to try to live off the grid! The town must be hard up for revenue. A Cape Coral woman cut off her own water and electricity in favor of rainwater that she collected and power from solar panels. However, a court magistrate ruled that Ms. Robin must use the city's water, and was given only a month to comply with the order.

*We wonder what she had been up to...*A woman was arrested for allegedly driving drunk – and without pants. When Pasco county deputies pulled over Kristi Steuben, 39, they could smell alcohol, officials reported. However, it wasn't until they asked her to step out of her car that they noticed that she was naked from the waist down.

Could we say the bond between this lady and her dog failed? A Tampa woman was arrested for using glue to close up her dog's Caesarian section. The dog had trouble giving birth, so she sliced the dog's stomach open.

The mama dog died and the woman was charged with animal cruelty. We learn that the pups lived.

It was only a drill? Police rushed in and Brandon Regional Hospital near Tampa went into lockdown when someone reported seeing a man with a gun in the halls. After a few minutes, police realized the supposed-gunman was a hospital maintenance man carrying a power drill. *What nincompoops!*

Bad break but he'll get three free hots and a cot! A drunken man showed up at a County jail to visit his girlfriend, then refused a deputy sheriff's instruction to depart at the end of his visit with her. The man said he would not leave and told the deputy that he would have to arrest him to get rid of him. That is just what the deputy did – arrest him. Now he is closer to his girlfriend.

This was a funny police report. It read, in part: "Police arrested a man for bringing a pussy into a strip joint." Managers at the Emerald City gentlemen's club in the town of

Murdock refused to allow Everett Lages, 47, and his pet kitten into the club. The intoxicated Lages became angry and telephoned 911. He was taken into custody for misuse of 911, trespassing and disorderly conduct. The kitten was put in the safe hands of animal control. *No pussies allowed in a strip joint – who knew?*

Freelance stripping? Clearwater Beach, Florida really does have some of the most beautiful, clear water of the entire Gulf Coast. It is a great little city with a wonderful people. Not too long ago, a Clearwater woman was arrested after she walked into the Baby Dolls gentlemen's club in Clearwater, took off her clothes, got on stage and started dancing for tips. Some gentlemen's clubs in other states actually encourage this kind of behavior. However, this is not the case in Florida. The woman, Nadia Botkins, was not employed by the club. It was the real dancers who called the police on her. She was arrested. The lesson to be learned: *No freelance stripping in Clearwater Beach?*

Gobble, Gobble... The headline read: "Next time he should practice his calls indoors." A hunter was good at making turkey calls, so good, in fact, that another hunter winged him with a shot in the woods near Tampa. The fellow hunter hit Clint Gale twice, but being a tough bird himself, Gale survived the shooting.

We might say there was big mischief afoot... Officials report that a woman stole one of Hulk Hogan's shoes, worth $5,500, from the wrestler's store in Clearwater Beach. The theft went down like a wrestling script. The woman's pals distracted the store clerks by pushing over a life-size statue of Hogan as she snatched the autographed shoe from a case. No arrest has yet been made.

It may be best not to try to take more than 10 items through the express checkout line when senior citizens are around. Violence broke out at a Fort Myers-area Walmart when a 77-year-old shopper attacked a 65-year-ol man who was scanning 20 items in the express aisle. The older man was not arrested, but continued to shake his clenched fist as he was escorted out after the beat down.

They were drunk, high and speeding away from a crime scene – but a new lawsuit says it's the tree's fault they crashed. The family of a woman who died in a fiery wreck is suing homeowners in a Tampa area neighborhood where she and her fellow suspect hit a tree during a high-speed chase and died. The suit contends the wreck was the homeowners' fault for failing to put up a warning sign near the tree. This is so ridiculous! The lawsuit should be thrown out of court forthwith... *"Failure to put a warning sign near the tree!"* Balderdash, Indeed!

Yep, the work of a numbskull! A fugitive took to Facebook recently to defend himself after the Pasco County Sheriff's office posted a picture of him with the label: "Fugitive of the Day." The posting offended robbery suspect, Matthew Oliver of New Port Richey, who commented about it on his own Facebook page that the wanted poster that the Sheriff's

Office had posted had slandered him. Two days later, police arrested him outside of his apartment. *What a great way to nab a hoodlum, eh...*

Could we say he just wanted to live the "high life" before going back to jail where he belonged? According to police, a homeless man in St. Petersburg allegedly stole $1,000 worth of liquor from a restaurant. He took the stolen booze to a park, poured shots and handed them to everyone in sight. Generous drinker, Randall Brown, was soon arrested – making it the 50th time he had been arrested.

Knife throwing went out with vaudeville! A Collier County woman incensed with her boyfriend's farting, allegedly threw a knife that cut his stomach. Deborah Ann Burns, 37, said long-time partner Willie Butler passed gas as he strolled to the kitchen. When Burns protested, Butler allegedly threw a knife at her, but missed. She took the knife and threw it at him – a direct hit to the tummy. She was arrested for assault. *Ouch!*

This is what happens when "inquiring minds would like to know." Florida police nabbed one of their own snooping on his ex-wife's boyfriend, a local TV news anchor and tennis star, Anna Kournikova. The Clearwater Police Department's Internal Affairs Bureau caught the police lieutenant accessing state motor vehicle records to obtain the addresses of 54 people not connected to any crimes. He is now facing demotion or termination.

*Poor, poor robotic Bambi...*Sarasota County Sheriff's deputies and Florida State Wildlife officers are going after poachers, planting a robotic deer to draw gunfire from unlicensed hunters. Authorities have already brought charges against Gerald Brown and Karen Brown, both 47, for hunting out of season and weapons charges after they allegedly fired on the fake deer from their car.

Ah greed – prosecutors call it embezzlement... A former office manager was arrested after she threw a surprise office birthday for her boss that led investigators to discover that she stole $180,000 from the business in Lee County. Ruth Amen handled billing and payroll, at Gulf to Bay Realty in Boca Grande, for more than a decade, and allegedly paid for the surprise party with company funds without permission.

*Talk about the luck of the Irish...*Miriam Tucker, 80, was one of 400 women attending a Tampa charity event, where each paid $20 for a flute of champagne and a chance to win a one-carat diamond which was placed in one of the glasses. She drank up and swallowed the winner! She already had a colonoscopy scheduled for soon after the charity event. The $5,000 diamond was recovered by her doctor during the colonoscopy.

Knucklehead!! A Tampa man allegedly made at least seven calls to 911 asking the dispatcher to send a female deputy, with whom he could have sex. Joshua was charged with making false calls to 911.

Bad Mommy! Bad, bad Mommy – but you look fabulous! A St. Petersburg police officer found it necessary to use his stun gun on a 19 year old woman who allegedly resisted arrest after leaving her 7 month old daughter in her car while she was sunning herself in a nearby tanning salon.

EL STUPIDO! A Tampa police employee was punished after running a personal errand in a department vehicle -- the police helicopter. The helicopter pilot reportedly took the chopper to the St. Petersburg airport to drop off fishing net to a friend of his.

BEEP BEEP! A Tampa woman unhappy with her son's grades made him stand at a busy intersection wearing a sign that read, "Honk if I need an education." A goodly number of motorists honked at the 15 year old. We learn, however, that the state child protection agency was not amused at the stunt. They are now investigating the mother.

This story reminds us that there is a "black market" for almost everything. Three Tampa area men were arrested recently for allegedly trying to sell stolen disposable diapers at an apartment complex. Police authorities surmise that the trio stole the diapers from a local Babies R US and then went to a nearby apartment complex to sell their swag. *DIAPERS! GET YOUR DIAPERS! DIAPERS HERE! DIAPERS CHEAP...*

Potato salad? We wonder what she would have done if he had refused to give her a piece of his steak. A Tampa woman grabbed a knife and threatened her 80 year old father when he refused to share his potato salad at dinner. His meal was interrupted when Karen Henry waved a blade in his face. Her dad grabbed a chair to defend himself. 911 was called. Karen was subsequently arrested.

Wonder why he needed 10 cans of deodorant? A suspected shoplifter created quite a "stink" when he grabbed 10 cans of deodorant and stuffed them in his pants said police in Sarasota. Pursued by a security guard, the 45-year-old man fled on a bicycle but was soon apprehended. *We still wonder why he needed 10 cans of deodorant?*

The headline read: "His sausage was showing." A naked man was caught on surveillance video stealing $15 worth of sausages, a first aid kit and a package of napkins from the club house of an apartment complex in Estero. The video linking him to the sausage theft showed him sneaking in wearing shorts, which he removed to take a shower before air drying himself.

An idiotic policy in light of all the hungry people in Florida. This story must have a hole in it. A Dunkin' Donuts worker in Florida who took home end of the day unsold pastries has been arrested for grand theft. A manager at the Newport Richey store pressed criminal charges after the employee defied a standing order to throw out the leftovers.

Heard of man bites dog? Well, in this one dog Tases policeman. The policeman accidently fired a Taser into his own leg after a suspect's dog jumped him. Officer Curtiss Richard reported that he was answering a domestic disturbance call when he drew his Taser. The dog bit his right forearm causing the self-inflicted wound. The dog, Buddy, a five year old mixed breed was impounded and sentenced to 10 days in quarantine.

Dummy! A Florida school teacher posted on his Facebook page that he hated his job and his students, and dreaded coming to work. It appears he got his wish. He received a five day suspension without pay for his posting. We've learned that the Manatee County School Board is now drafting rules that will restrict teachers' conduct with respect to online social media.

Hiding in plain site? A 21 year old man with outstanding burglary arrest warrants hanging over his head lied about his age and enrolled in a Tampa middle school and even managed to play for the football team. Julious Threatts played in the season opener after claiming to be 14. He was arrested after another school telephoned and advised he had pulled the same deception there.

KA-CHING! Here's one about dirty money. A DWI and drug suspect in Florida surprised police when $45 fell out of his behind during a strip search. Nicholas H, 19, who initially denied he had any cash on him, was described by police as being like a human ATM machine. *KA-CHING!*

Chapter Three:

Dumbest Central Florida Criminals

Professor Birdsong has had the privilege of travelling all over Florida, but he loves his home in Orlando the best. Central Florida is full of attractions, Disney World, Universal Studios, and Sea World, that draw a lot of tourists but he never wants to live anywhere else. Oh yeah…and they're lots of dumb criminals here, too…See for yourself:

***

Yes, prayer can move mountains! Patrick W had his 3-year-old son in his car when he was pulled over in Daytona Beach to solicit a prostitute who turned out to be an undercover police officer. Mr. W is fighting the "solicitation" charges. His defense is that he "only pulled over to pray for the young lady who he thought had strayed from the church."

Hoodoo Voodoo! Were there zombies and the walking dead in the ring? Central Florida authorities recently announced the arrest of members of a meth ring that actually employed a voodoo priest. The voodoo priest served as a "spiritual adviser" to the ring's reputed leader "El Don" Florence. The takedown of the ring was dubbed operation Hoodoo Voodoo.

It certainly was some sort of weird homicide! Here's a weird and tragic story from DeLand. Marlon Brown, 38, was pulled over by police for not wearing his seatbelt. Dash-cam video from the police car showed that Brown got out his car and began to run. The police officer gave chase in his police cruiser and ran over and killed Brown. The manner of death was ruled an accident, however, the Florida Department of Law Enforcement Medical Examiners Commission has called the autopsy report into question. Although a grand jury did not indict Officer James Harris of any wrongdoing, he was fired and settlement was reached with the Brown family who received $500,000 from the city of DeLand. Brown's wife, Krystal contends that officer Harris should be charged with vehicular homicide.

Just how many bras can one woman wear at a time? A dragnet conducted by the Seminole County Sheriff's office just before Christmas 2013 resulted in 48 arrests, including a woman charged with stealing $1,700 worth of bras from a shopping mall. A part of the dragnet was comprised of plain-clothes deputy detectives who worked undercover inside a number of different stores.

Merry Christmas! Speeding drivers in Melbourne were stunned on Christmas day, 2013, when police issued them scratch-off lottery tickets instead of traffic tickets. Police in the holiday spirit bought the lottery tickets with their own money and handed them out along with warnings to drivers caught speeding or making other traffic violations

*So humane....*A bandit carjacked a woman in a dangerous crime-ridden section of Orlando, but he didn't want to leave her defenseless in that part of town. So, he handed her a box cutter to defend herself from other possible criminals. He then said, "take care of yourself" and drove away in her Honda vehicle.

The headline read: "Plan goes sour: Man arrested in thefts" An 81-year-old man allegedly stole 11 truckloads of tangerines a few weeks ago and sold them, at a market for more than $300, according to Polk County deputy sheriffs. Henry South got away with it, they said. However, the next day he went back to the same farm and stole an additional 2,000 tangerines or more, deputies maintained. But this time he was not so lucky. South and another man were found at the farm by the Polk County Sheriff's Office of Aviation unit and arrested. South was taken to jail and given an $8,500 bond on charges of grand theft or more than 2,000 pieces of citrus and trespassing. *Only in FloriDUH!*

Assault with a dangerous weapon – rocky road. A Port St. Lucie woman spotted her cheating husband at a Walgreens drug store with his side girlfriend, so she attacked him with a tub of ice cream she had just purchased. We hear that the cheating husband was bruised and hurt while his wife was arrested on an assault charge. The ice cream was rocky road.

The headline read: "His plans fell through." Police responded to a silent alarm at a CVS pharmacy in Melbourne and found a maintenance hatch open. Moments later, a ski mask wearing man fell out of the hatch right in front of the police. An arrest was immediately made.

I'll bet that hooch was a lot cheaper than orange flavored Ciroc... Polk County sheriff's deputies broke up an illegal distillery in Haines City that brewed moonshine in creative flavors, such as peach and apple, deputies report.

A Fort Pierce man, depressed because he had no one with whom to celebrate his birthday, ended up with lots of company – in the police station. The birthday man called 911 to complain that his neighbor wouldn't drink with him to celebrate. Police explained to him that he was misusing 911. When he called again, they came to his house and arrested him.

Cheep, cheep, cheep – cheaper than a lawsuit! We have learned that an autistic Florida boy will be allowed to keep his chickens. J.J. Hart loved his chickens which brought joy to his life and halted his temper tantrums. His mother had given him his first chicken and it had a soothing effect on him. However, after a local law allowing people to keep chickens at home expired, officials proceeded to remove the chickens. After his parents threatened to sue, the City Council of DeBarry voted to let J.J. keep his chickens at their home.

Temper, temper! Maria Desimone, 45, was arrested at a Walmart in Palm Bay after she allegedly flipped out over the price of a skateboard she had hoped to buy as a Christmas present. Desimone threatened to kill the sales manager and swung the expensive skateboard at the sales manager. Police were called...

Doesn't sound like a satisfying wedding night does it... This one is about a marriage that did not get off to a good start. A newlywed in Orlando called police when her new husband went missing from their honeymoon hotel suite. Police found him when he met up with a "hooker" – who turned out to be an undercover detective on an anti-prostitution detail.

*Yes, love will find a way...*A police officer in Ocoee could be banned from wearing a badge after his bosses found that he used the 911 system to arrange trysts with his mistress. Officer S. W. allegedly had his lover call 911 and hang up so he would be dispatched to her location.

We learn that a Walmart assistant manager has been fired for turning his work day into an action movie. Mel C, an assistant manager at the store in Titusville, risked his life to stop a beer thief by jumping in the back of the bandit's getaway pickup truck and riding with him for 15 miles. Mr. C eventually flagged down another driver, who pulled a gun on the thief. Yes, the beer was recovered but what a cost.

...Seems he was more likely to have been a monkey's uncle! Daylen Holloman, 20, was recently approached by a Daytona Beach policeman responding to a call about a suspicious person at a 7-Eleven. "I know I'm a monkey," Holloman told the officer. When the officer said, "You're human because you wear clothes," Holloman stripped naked. He was then arrested.

D'OH! A bandit at a gas station in Ocala asked to fill out a job application as a ruse to make clerks drop their guard. He then reached into the cash registers while they weren't looking and made off with a wad of bills.

Accused thief, Anthony Thomas, was soon caught. How and Why? Because he was foolish enough to fill out the job application with his true name and address.

Yet, another terrorist in the making... A 16-year-old Florida high school girl, who teachers maintain is an exemplary student, has been hit with a felony charge for what she claimed was a "science experiment." Kiera Wilmot mixed household cleaning liquids in a bottle, which exploded on school grounds. No one was injured. Nevertheless, she was charged with "discharging a destructive device." In her defense, she said she expected only smoke and not a blast.

Can we say he was "relieved" before he was arrested? A Florida burglar was arrested after he stopped to play with a toy helicopter and snack on a salad in a home, according to police. Jason Lee Vickery, 23, even went to the bathroom for some personal time.

We're sure they wanted to do more than just say hi! A woman called police near Orlando after she escaped from two men who had jumped from a van and chased her down the street. When investigators found and questioned the men, they said they had been so impressed with the woman, that they just wanted to say hi – but that she was too fast.

Amen! An allegedly acid-crazed Florida college student pleaded with police not to cut off his penis, then abruptly changed his mind and begged them to sever his member. The police refused, deciding to Taser him, instead. The student still managed to punch one of the officers in the head. He then proclaimed that he was "God." Unfortunately, God was sent to lock up. *Amen!*

HALLELULAH!!! At a gas station in suburban Orlando, a woman began shouting that she was "God," doused her car with gasoline and set it ablaze with a lighter. A witness recued two dogs from the burning car. "God" was taken into custody for a mental evaluation.

Polk County Sheriff's deputies didn't drag "their heels." Why not? Because when they arrested an alleged foot fetishist, who reportedly told them that since the age of 16, he had approached hundreds of women asking to touch their toes or feet. Reginald C, 23, said he used ruses such as telling them that he was trying to earn a Boy Scout community service badge, or that he was a college student doing medical research. *Little pervert...*

She may be a hero, but a dumb one – call animal control! A Lake County woman helped to make her children's walk home from school safer – by wrestling an alligator. Jessica McGregor spotted the gator shuffling toward Clermont Middle School and lassoed it with a rope, jumped on its back and held its mouth shut. This heroic mother just so happens to be a deputy sheriff.

Nitwit! A thief at a Deland Dunkin' Donut asked the cashier for a pen, sat down at a table and wrote a holdup note on a napkin, went back to counter and got away with money from the cash drawer. Police said he indicated that he had a gun, but he may have forgotten to bring that too.

We would say he was a not so "Sharp" nitwit... A Florida man pretended he was an officer of the law for five months – because he was too embarrassed to admit to his girlfriend he was really a pizza delivery man. Christopher Sharp would leave his pizza shop each day, put on a sheriff deputy's uniform and head over to his girl's house, where he would regale her with phony stories of chasing and arresting bad guys. Sharp was eventually arrested for stalking and posing as a deputy.

Hot 2 Trot? A woman in Fort McCoy refused to pull over when police attempted to stop her for driving too fast. When police were able to apprehend her, she told them that she had been too embarrassed to stop because she was topless. She added that she had been speeding because she was in a rush to surprise her boyfriend.

He is, of course, a stupid pyromaniac! A man marked the one year anniversary of his arson arrest with another arrest --- for setting the vacant house next door ablaze. James B, on probation after his arson conviction last year, allegedly called dispatchers to report the fire next door in New Smyrna Beach.

Wow, we wonder what he did to provoke this kind of mayhem? Police in New Smyrna Beach say a woman gave her ex-husband a shock – and then some! She allegedly used a stun gun on him, tied him to the bumper of a pickup truck, and dragged him for a half-mile. Robert Hall, 54, wound up in the hospital. His ex-wife, along with two friends who took part in the attack, face attempted murder charges.

Yep, sounds just like Florida... A Florida vigilante, in a crowded Walmart parking lot, opened fire on a suspected shoplifter's car. Jose Martinez told police he saw the alleged crook stealing steaks and blasted four rounds into the fleeing suspect's trunk to "mark" the car for police. Martinez had a gun license, but was arrested, basically for stupidity.

It is seldom pretty when East meets West. Three masked gunmen burst into the New China restaurant in Orlando and demanded money. However, the Chinese employees could not understand the robbers, who then banged on the cash register to indicate what they wanted. Nothing! They didn't understand. The frustrated crooks gave up and fled. Police with a police dog soon caught and arrested the suspects.

*Sounds like the handy work of some University of Central Florida fraternity boys to me...*An Orlando man got a scare when he glanced into some woods and spotted an 800 pound gorilla. Then, shock set in, when he learned that the realistic looking ape was a life-size $5,000 bronze statue of a silverback gorilla that someone had dumped in a wooded area after stealing it from a nearby hotel.

There's no idiot like a hungry idiot.... Donald Delong, 21, allegedly pulled a pellet gun on a

McDonald's drive-thru employee in St. Cloud. The worker had told Delong that the drive-thru had just closed. The employee called the police who arrested the hungry Delong at the Pizza Hut next door.

Dumkopf! A Florida man is blaming his DWI arrest on President Obama's re-election. Reginald Robertson, 52, reportedly claimed he was arrested because he is an African American, and the white police officer was angry over Obama's victory. However, the fact that he had been driving 35 mph over the speed limit and said, "I had too much to drink" may have also been factors in his arrest.

Sounds like the police have finally caught on ... A homeless Florida man allegedly cheated Disney World out of $18,000 by using the same stolen credit card scheme at least two dozen times, police report. Jeffrey Hawkins, 49, allegedly told police, "it's easy to commit fraud at Disney, and I've been then here a lot."

No such luck, they were in fact thieves! A Reddick motorist arriving home was shocked to find that rock-hardened crooks had made off with 800 square feet of pricey paving stones from her driveway. Neighbors who witnessed the theft, which took place over several hours, said they assumed the thieves had been hired by the homeowner.

KA-BOOOOOM, birdbrains.... It has been reported that two Florida men helping a friend to move were seriously hurt after they ignored a gas leak warning. Lit cigarettes in hand, Jose Alvarado and a friend walked toward an apartment and set off a huge explosion.

He was a thief and a freeloader too. A Florida woman was dismayed to discover that her house had been broken in to. But, she became outraged to find that the burglar had gone into her kitchen, toasted some "Eggos" and enjoyed them with syrup. Police assume that the breakfast must have given the bandit some energy, because he made off with

$3,800 in goods. He was later caught and arrested.

Little cretin... A Florida teenager was arrested recently for calling 911 to tell police about a dream. Mike W, 18, reportedly told the dispatcher, "Everything that happened today is actually in my dream, and I want to prove it to everybody." An officer went to his house and advised him not to call again. He called anyway, and was arrested.

The Wild West is alive and well in Bunnell! Police in Bunnell had to "corral" a drunken man who took them on a half-hour chase – while riding his horse. Chuck Cole, 29, told the officers who tried to pull him over that he was on his way to see his grandmother. He refused orders to dismount, and reared the horse back and took off. The horse got tired after 30 minutes of galloping and stopped, allowing police to arrest Cole.

Ironic. No? A Florida couple allegedly left three of their five young children home alone, so they could get married. Kimberly F, 30, and Daniel P, 34, allegedly headed for the courthouse in a rush after P learned that he would have to pay child support if he did not get married. Now, they have no children to support – they were taken away by child protective services. *Ironic. No?*

OUCH! A Port Orange gas station attendant used cans of Natural Ice beer to thwart a would be robber who tried to steal cash from the register. When the robber put down the knife he had been waving and reached for the cash, the clerk beaned him with a couple of cans of beer.

A Florida convenience store featured one stop shopping for drug users. The store in Edgewater sold bath salts and marijuana, as well as "clean" urine to beat drug tests. People subjected to "pee in this cup" drug tests can deliver clean urine with a "device" worn beneath clothing. What kind of device? The "device" is called a "Whizzanator."

Her motive was clearly to be sent back to jail for the next several months! A 45-year-old woman with an arrest history for minor crimes was arrested again recently after children told police she exposed herself to them, as they played touch football outside a youth center in New Smyrna Beach. Dale Delgado Wisniewski pulled down her jeans in front of about nine children ages 7 to 14, police report. Police could not speculate on her motive. While at the police station Wisniewski struck an officer and was rearrested on a felony battery charge. She remains in jail in lieu of a $24,000 bond.

Such a deal, I'm telling you, only 20 bucks. The old saying goes: "crime doesn't pay," but in Florida, criminals might have to pay. A Florida appellate court has just ruled that every new convict has to come up with $20 to support Crime Stopper programs.

Boy, oh boy, you can still run but it's getting harder to hide! The Polk County Sheriff's Office has launched a mobile app – the first of its kind among Central Florida law enforcement agencies. The FLPolkSO app, available for Apple and Android devices, features mug shots of sex offenders and the area's most wanted suspects. The "Most Wanted" and "Sex Offenders" buttons list images alphabetically or allow users to search by first name, last name, age and gender. The FLPolkSO app also lets users register for the Victim Information and Notification Network (VINE), which alerts users if a particular offender is released from jail or prison. Users can also email crime tips to the Sheriff's office.

Who claims there are no benefits to "Obamacare?" A Florida inmate admitted to a judge that his threat to kill president Obama was a bid to remain incarcerated and receive medical treatment in Prison. Career criminal, Stephen E, 57, uses a wheel chair and had received chemotherapy in federal custody. He is expected to undergo heart surgery in prison. In 2001 Mr. E had also issued a death threat against then—President George W. Bush—and served 18 months.

Who knew carjackers were so dumb! Two thieves in Orlando forced a Corvette owner out of his expensive sports car at gunpoint – but they did not know how to put the manual transmission into drive. The owner recounted, with the handgun pointed at his head, "I had to tell the driver four different times to push the clutch." Apparently not knowing what a clutch was, the robbers fled on foot.

Don Selvage is Lakeland city commissioner who is working overtime to repeal a 69-year-old law that bans spitting on public sidewalks or grass. Although the town has handed out only 117 spitting tickets since 2000, Selvage has put forth his "Expectoration Proclamation," in reaction to the injustice of a man being charged for spitting last year. *PA TOOOTIE...*

Bad, bad, bad mommy! Spring Hill police arrested a 31-year old mother who passed out drunk on her couch, allowing her 10-year old son to drink liquor and wander outside with no clothes.

Slinging pies can be dangerous work! A loyal Papa John's deliverer in Daytona refused to hand over $26 in pies to a robber and held them tight even after the bandit zapped him with a stun gun. The deliverer was not badly hurt and police soon arrested a suspect.

It's time for him to think about retiring. We do not slap students for kissing – even in Florida. A Cocoa school teacher who was a finalist for last year's Teacher of the Year Award was suspended for 20 days after he slapped a female student for kissing in a school hallway. The teacher had a clean record and had been on the job since the 1970s.

YIKESSSS!!!! Fort Pierce: A car thief broke into a van in Fort Pierce, apparently not realizing the van belonged to a funeral home. As the thief drove along, he noticed he was sharing his ride with the corpse of a dead 98 year old woman. He became so unnerved at the sight that he ditched the van just two blocks away and ran off. No arrest has been made.

Yes, there are fake police out there, believe it or not. Listen to this one. Real Sheriffs' deputies in Orange County, Florida, arrested a pair of imposters, who happened to be brothers, after one of them pulled over a motorist on a highway while driving a real looking police car, complete with lights and sirens, authorities report. As police deputies were arresting the first phony officer, a second one drove up on the scene in his identical fake car to give his brother back up. Police report that they were both arrested.

OK! First, no more "24 hour parties" with hookers. After a 47 year old man was shot in the chest by an AK-47 at an Orlando motel, doctors patching up his wound found a tumor in his lung and removed it. The man who had been shot during a "24 hour party" with hookers said he wants to use his second chance to turn his life around. *OK! First, no more "24 hour parties" with hookers.*

They could also be charged with assault with a deadly weapon – baby! Sheriff's deputies arrested two suspected shoplifters at an

Orlando Walmart after one of them used a baby's car seat to take swing at one of the arresting deputies. Unfortunately, the baby was still strapped in the baby seat. Jodie Willis, 25, and Megan Kelley, 21, were both arrested and charged with robbery and child neglect. It was Kelley's baby who Willis allegedly used as a weapon.

Smart was not very smart. What can you do with a Lake Eola Swan, anyway? An Orlando man was arrested for allegedly stealing a swan from a park. A witness saw Geffre Smart, 24, take the swan from Lake Eola Park, police report. The witness called police, who followed a trail of feathers to Smart's home. It was further reported that the swan was not injured and Smart was charged with theft and cruelty to animals.

Ouch! This one is about a man facing assault charges for assaulting his girlfriend with a grilled cheese sandwich. It appears that the assault occurred when a furious Todd Harvey allegedly mashed the sandwich into Amanda

Fulford's face. Hungry for revenge, she tried to bite off his tongue. *They are both idiots!*

Look for the suspect under the sea. Osceola County Sheriff's deputies are looking for a thief who was dressed like SpongeBob SquarePants as he robbed a 7-Eleven in the Orlando area. The police report advises that the suspect did not completely buy into the role because he only wore the SpongeBob mask. We learn there were no SquarePants worn.

OK! We get it...support her...bras for support. Yuk, yuk. A man loves his incarcerated girlfriend so much he shoplifted two bras for her as a gift, police report. Now Johnnie B, 29, is behind bars as his girlfriend prepares to get out of jail in a few days. After Mr. B was nabbed at WalMart he allegedly told police, "She has done so much for me... I felt I had to support her."

Wow! What a sentence. Timothy Raymond Anderson, 51, had been arrested in 2008 on child sex charges by Palm Bay police. In

September, 2010, a jury convicted him of the sexual battery charges. Judge Dan Vaughn then sentenced him to 999 years, 99 months, and 98 days in prison. Authorities arrested Anderson after an investigation revealed that he had abused a girl from 1988 to 1991 on a near daily basis, beginning when she was six years old and in his care.

She was lucky they didn't "bust" her in the mouth. The Orlando Sentinel reported that police are on the lookout for two men who robbed a woman at gunpoint. According to police, a woman sitting in a car was approached by two men with T-shirts covering their faces who demanded money. The woman told them she had no money, so they opened the door and demanded her purse. She advised that she did not have her purse with her. At this point the police report maintains that one of the men then reached in her bra and took $70 and fled.

Criminal Barbering? Veteran's Day weekend, 2010, the Orange County Sheriff's department became a national laughingstock when it was reported that sheriff deputies and members of the Florida Department of Business and Professional Regulation carried out a series of warrantless raids against local Orlando barbershops that made history for arresting 35 people on misdemeanor charges of "barbering without a license," after having spent several months investigating the matter. A records check revealed that in the last ten years only three people in the entire state of Florida went to jail on such charges. In the instant cases, many of the warrantless sweeps entailed officers swarming the barbershops that had children inside and putting the barbers in handcuffs and "perp walking" them to police vehicles. We learn that one felony arrest was made when one of the raids netted a barber with an unlicensed handgun. We learn further that all the barbershops were in the African American and Hispanic neighborhoods. *Obviously, those neighborhoods are "hotbeds" of criminal barbering.*

Chapter Four:

Dumbest South Florida Criminals

South Florida has South Beach in Miami and Fort Lauderdale has the famous beach where the movie "Where the Boys Are," was filmed long ago. These beaches provide great fun. My youngest daughter went to college in Miami; boy, did she really love living down there. However, if you think there were some pretty dumb criminals in Central Florida – just wait and see how dumb these south Florida criminals can be. Really dumb... Please read on...

***

You can look but do not date them. A 76-year-old man broke his 77-year-old wife's hip in a rowdy fight when she discovered him looking at a dating website. "She accused me of cheating and was yelling at me, so I pushed her," Edward Aronson admitted after his wife of 33 years was hospitalized following the fight at their Lake Worth home.

And, the hospital will soon welcome a malpractice lawsuit from the couple. A doctor and nurses abandoned a woman in labor, leaving her and her husband to deliver their baby. Indira and Zamir Andahary were at a Boynton Beach hospital, just after midnight on a Sunday morn when the team left to perform an emergency Caesarian. The nurse allegedly said, "You have to wait and hold it. The doctor is busy with a C-section and that takes priority over you," Zamir said. The couple soon welcomed their healthy daughter into the world.

A lazy, lazy thief failed to knock over a Wendy's in Miramar when he tried to hold it up from inside his car at the drive through window. Although he had a gun, the clerk simply closed the service window and went to call police. The would-be robber drove away but was soon caught and arrested. *Nit Wit!!*

"V" for Vendetta or victim? An off duty North Miami Beach police officer was arrested at an Obamacare protest rally in Plantation for refusing to take off a "Guy Fawkes" mask. Ericson Harrell, 39, was wearing a cape and the mast at the rally that has been popularized by the film "V for Vendetta," and often worn by Occupy Wall Street protestors. He allegedly refused to identify himself or show his face when officers asked him to. We understand that he is now on leave from the North Miami Police department. He probably now thinks "V" is for "victim" of Obamacare.

Gators aren't legal currency! Fernando Aguilera was arrested after he went into a Miami convenience store and tried to trade a live 4-foot alligator for a 12 pack of beer. The clerk called police and Aguilera was charged with violating Florida wildlife laws.

No good deed goes unpunished! A group of church people were kicked out of a Lake Worth park for trying to help the homeless on Thanksgiving Day, 2014. The church folks had started giving away turkey and stuffing when police ordered them to stop the handouts. The church people were very surprised and, one of them said "We were there to feed people that just don't get a nice warm meal like the rest of us."

Yep, again no good deed goes unpunished! A Fort Lauderdale woman was arrested for calling 911 to report a bunch of drunken people– at a bar. Mary Jaggers was reportedly charged with abusing the 911 system, for allegedly repeatedly telephoning to report that there were too many drunks at Arties Sportsman Lounge. As Jaggers was taken away by police, she maintained she only wanted to prevent drunken driving.

A Boynton Beach motorist was so mad while a police officer was writing her an "unbuckled seat belt" ticket that she call 911 to complain, and was arrested for doing so. Misusing 911 is misdemeanor punishable up to a year in jail in Florida. *Guess she never heard "click it or ticket."*

They also probably didn't get any tips. A gaggle of parking valets at a cruise ship port in Miami unleashed their frustrations at not being paid for parking the cars for all the passengers on an entire cruise ship. How? They dumped all of the passengers' car keys into a random pile after a dispute with their bosses. The drivers were stranded for hours as they sorted through the hundreds of car keys.

How stupid! This one sure saved everyone a lot of time. Three women were arrested after showing up for a Florida drug hearing with drugs on them. Among them, they had dozens of pills and a syringe, as well as a tourniquet. All three were there to give urine samples to prove they were keeping up with their court-ordered drug treatment. *And yes, this was in Miami!*

With her temper, deportation may probably be best! A lovely, but hot tempered young woman was arrested on domestic violence charges Karole Pitcherski, 24, an undocumented Polish citizen allegedly began beating, choking and scratching her current boyfriend after he said no when she asked him to marry her. Karole had reportedly been hoping that getting married in a lovely June wedding would get her that green card that she so desperately hoped to earn. She was quite upset that she might get deported back to Poland. *However, if she casts her net a bit wider Karole may, also soon learn that there are a lot more fish in the sea of men who might wish to marry her.*

We now have the legalized use of "chin-prints" in Florida. Elena Victoria of the wealthy town of Boca Raton leaped out of her car after drunkenly crashing. She was coming from a summer cocktail party. She claimed she had not been behind the wheel. Police, however, found what looked like her chin print in the soft foam of her steering wheel. They then saw a wound on her chin and decided to arrest her for DWI. *Caught by the prints of her little chiny chin, chin...*

You might say she was "carted" off to the slammer. A woman was arrested for repeatedly dialing 911 after a supermarket worker tried to retrieve the shopping cart in which she was sitting. Catherine Day of Boca Raton refused to relinquish the Publix Supermarket cart and called 911 when the worker confronted her, she dialed again when police arrived and told her to give up the cart, and a third time when police returned to tell her to stop calling 911.

A Miami area woman was arrested for alleged misuse of 911, calling police looking to hook up with an officer she had just met. Mary Colon, 48, originally called police over a civil dispute about a car. And, then she turned her attention to the responding officer, authorities said, telling him: "I am so horny."

Did the clock also tell the time? Police in Lake Worth, armed with batons and stun guns, took at least ten minutes to subdue a crazed young man who had stripped off all his clothes and entered another person's home. The 17-year-old, who was wielding a clock, "which had numerous sharp utensils protruding" from it, was charged with burglary, criminal mischief and battery.

Looks like the big sacker got sacked! New York Giants pro bowl defensive tackle Shaun Rogers picked up a woman recently in a Miami Beach night spot and brought her back to his room in the Fontainebleau – where she, apparently, waited for him to go to sleep and then stole $500,000 of his jewelry. The 6-4, 350 pounder told police he was out partying with a man and a woman and easily won over a woman he met in the club. The couple and the second woman escorted Rogers back to his hotel room. Upon arrival he immediately stashed his jewelry in the room safe. And eventually went to sleep while the others kept partying. When he woke, his date had disappeared. He tried to get in the safe but couldn't get the door open. Hotel security was able to open the safe and found most of Rogers' bling missing.

There will be no second date. A first date in Boynton Beach went wrong when a 19-yearold "perfect gentleman" took a woman for a stroll on the beach, and then pulled a gun on her in the parking lot of a fast food restaurant and stole her car. The victim called

911 and police captured the so-called "perfect gentleman."

It appears from the naked attack on the Rottweiler that Delice might have moved up from pot to PCP... A naked Miami man jumped into a neighbor's yard and began choking a chained Rottweiler, whose owner came out and shot the fellow in the foot. A wild Jeffrey Delice, 20, then tried to assault the homeowner, who held him at bay for police. Police investigating the attack say Delice has never been convicted of a crime, but last year was charged with possession of marijuana,

So dumb... A Miami area public defender was fired after she posted photos of her client's leopard print underwear on Facebook. The racy undies had been sent to the client, an accused killer, by his girlfriend to wear at trial. The judge in the case also declared a mistrial in the case.

Early last year a Fort Lauderdale Judge sentenced a man who had an altercation with his wife to take her out on a "date" that included elegant dining at the local Red Lobster followed by a night of bowling. Judge John Hurley also ordered defendant Joseph Bray "to stop somewhere and get some flowers" for his wife. *We're sure that "somewhere for flowers" was the Publix Grocery store! What a cheap date...*

The rubber probably cleanses the taste of carrion from the vultures' palates. It has been reported that recently vultures in Everglades National Park have somehow acquired a taste for rubber – and are attacking parked cars, ripping off their windshield wipers and dining on the blades. The problem has become so serious that park rangers are giving visitors tarps to drape around their vehicles.

Big mouth kids need to be shut up, but it was only a misdemeanor conviction. A Florida man was arrested after police pulled him over and his 7-year old told the officers that the women in the back seat of the car were prostitutes. "Those are my daddy's hos'," the boy reportedly said. The father, Robert Burton was convicted of being a pimp.

Jesus! What next? A woman running for mayor of North Miami this last election season put up posters declaring she "is endorsed by Jesus Christ." Candidate Anna Pierre even had a picture of the Son of God on the ad. The "endorsement" didn't work with voters – she finished at the bottom in a field of seven candidates. *Jesus! What next?*

We guess the two house crime spree made him thirsty! A 21-year-old suspected burglar fleeing from police still managed time for a beer break. Police pursued him from one home to another in Lighthouse Point in Broward County. He was arrested as he emerged from the second house carrying two bottles of Heineken.

Sounds like bad karma for that thief... A man was arrested for buying drinks at a Miami Beach bar with a stolen credit card that turned out to belong to the bartender. The suspect had taken the credit card from the bartender's car which was parked at a nearby garage. The stunned bartender immediately called police.

Ana, you are such a schmuck for using your children this way! A South Florida mother who brought her five children along for the ride when she staged car crashes to make cash will spend even longer in prison because she put her children in harm's way, a judge has ruled. Ana Orlando was already facing a four year prison term. Instead she will spend 6 ½ years in a federal lockup. Orlando, 43, of Lake Worth, wept as her children, ages 3 to 16 at the time of the accidents, tearfully told the judge how much they want her home from prison.

BURP! A Palm Springs couple, apparently, paid for their prescription pill habit by shoplifting and selling infant formula. Sonya Barbour, 32, and Glen Martin, 31, were caught trying to sneak two dozen cans of formula out of a Walmart. Police also found 117 cans of formula in the couple's car. Their 9-month old son was put in the custody of Florida's Department of Children and

Families.

Slithery Dee you had better flee, bounty hunters want to kill thee! Officials in south Florida put out a call for people who want to go to the Everglades and shoot Burmese pythons, and more than 4,000 gunslinger wannabes signed up. The state is offering a $1,500 bounty to the "latter day St. Patrick" who removes the most of the nuisance snakes from the Everglades.

*Bow Wow...*A dog in Sebring riding in the back of his master's pickup truck stepped on a pistol that the guy had left there. The weapon discharged, and the man was slightly wounded. However, the doggie is off the hook -- police have declared the shooting an accident.

*Officials say they won't extradite him. Sounds like overkill anyway....*The federal case against a Miami doctor, charged with illegally selling drugs online, was dropped in part because there was so much evidence that it became too costly to keep track of it. The federal prosecutors had amassed 400,000 documents and two tetra bytes of electronic data against Armando Angulo, who is believed to be at large in Panama. *Officials there say they won't extradite him. Sounds like overkill anyway....*

*Ridiculous – No bail for failing to pay $85...Oh yeah, she was 23 years overdue! My bad...*A Disney dream cruise ended in a bad dream for a Connecticut woman over a shoplifting arrest 22 years ago. Robin Hall, 41, who works for aerospace manufacturer Pratt & Whitney, was arrested as she left the ship in Florida when federal officials conducting routine security checks found the open warrant for her 1991 arrest for allegedly having failed to pay $85 in court costs. She was being held without bail.

The headline read: "If you are going to be a squatter, think big." Andre Barbosa, 23, moved into a vacant, five bedroom, $2.5 million home in Boca Raton, claiming the foreclosed residence under Florida's "deed of adverse possession' law. Bewildered police decided to leave Barbosa alone in the house and let the bank holding the mortgage fight it out with Barbosa in court. *If you are gonna squat – squat big Barbosa. Squat big!*

Hair today, gone tomorrow! Esther Armstead, 20, allegedly tried to get away with stealing $1,620 from a hotel in Hollywood by hiding it in her wig. Esther glued the hairpiece onto her head with 15 $100 bills and 6 $20 bills stuck under it before police arrested her.

This is so stupid! Just try to collect from the deceased. A woman was issued a red light camera ticket three months after she died. Her sister Irene Lieberman, a County Commissioner, attempted to clear up the matter. Unfortunately, she learned, to her dismay, that death is not on the list of exceptions that allow the ticket to be quashed.

This story puts a new spin on the words "High School," No? Police arrested a South Plantation High School student after he allegedly brought marijuana laced cookies to campus and shared the chocolate chip delights with two classmates. The suspect's class mates had no idea they were being "treated" to pot.

L'Enfant Terrible! Talk about a food fight! When a 17-year-old hurled a water bottle at a cafeteria worker, hundreds of teens at Cypress Bay High School in Weston, began flinging chunks of lunch food at everyone in sight. When the fight spilled outside, it attracted hundreds of spectators and the police. The police arrested the original bottle thrower for striking a school administrator and for resisting arrest.

Hocus Pocus... A police officer and a police department employee got into trouble after they allegedly tried to get rid of the town's new cost cutting city manager by sprinkling bird seed around his office as part of a Santeria rite. The duo hoped that the ritual would make the manager quit before he could institute budget cuts.

Damned if she do and damned if she don't....
A Florida city manager who was fired for undergoing a sex change operation is in trouble at her new job. Why? It has been alleged that she is a homophobe. After being fired Susan Stanton became a hero to the gay and transgender communities, and found a job in the opened minded town of Lake Worth. However after she criticized a gay bar owner over a noise issue, activists called her anti-gay and demanded she be fired.

BOOM? A woman was arrested after she drew a picture of a bomb and wrote the word "Boom" on her friend's suitcase as a prank before the friend left for the Miami airport. The friend tried to check the bag with the bomb picture on it. This caused a major airport alert. The friend was not arrested but we are uncertain whether she made her flight.

Wow – just imagine how expensive a settlement it might have been if the bus driver had been eating caviar? A Jamaican beef patty cost a Florida county a pretty penny. A bus driver chowing down on the patty lost control of the bus, slammed down on the brakes and sent a dozen passengers sprawling to the floor. One of the passengers who was seriously injured settled with Broward County for $100,000.

*What a loser...*A Tamarac man on a mission to steal toys from all 50 states was finally arrested after more than a decade of stealthy shoplifting that he used to pay for his vacations — including a trip to Hawaii. Ignatius Polara, 46, would allegedly steal from toy shops and then sell the stolen goods on eBay.

If one wishes to bribe their way out of trouble it is best to have a lot of money. We learn that a drunken bicyclist in Boynton Beach found that out the hard way after he was arrested for pedaling while intoxicated and he tried to bribe the arresting officers. He first contended he was a "professional MMA cage fighter," and then told the police, "fifty cents to let me go." The cops just laughed. When in the heck did it become illegal to pedal a bike when drunk? *This is not driving while impaired under the statute!*

This is so weird...butt lifts performed in a motel room! The headline read: "She wasn't just a phony plastic surgeon; she was also a phony woman." A man was arrested in Palm Beach for allegedly giving people illegal butt enhancements without a license – and while posing as a woman. The victim's first hint that something might have been wrong should have come when the suspect preformed the bogus lifts in a motel room. *Butt lifts???*

The End

About the Author

Professor Birdsong received his J.D. from the Harvard Law School and his B.A. from Howard University. He teaches law in Orlando, Florida.

After graduation from law school, he worked four years at the law firm of Baker Hostetler. He then entered into a varied and distinguished career in government service. He served as a diplomat with the U.S. State Department with various postings in Nigeria, Germany and the Bahamas.

Professor Birdsong later served as a federal prosecutor. After leaving government service, and before he began teaching, Professor Birdsong was in private law practice in Washington, D.C.

www.BirdsongsLaw.com
lbirdsong@barry.edu

Leonard Birdsong

Ordering Information

New books coming soon!

Dear Reader,

If you liked this book, I would greatly appreciate you writing me a review on Amazon or any other book site.

I look forward to sharing more funny stories with you in future books.

Thank you, I really appreciate your help.

Regards,

Professor Birdsong

Winghurst Publications
1969 S. Alafaya Trail / Suite 303
Orlando, FL 32828-8732
www.BirdsongsLaw.com
lbirdsong@barry.edu

Leonard Birdsong

Other Books by Professor Birdsong:

* Professor Birdsong's 147 Dumbest Criminal Stories: Florida

* 177 Dumbest Criminal Stories – International

* Professor Birdsong's 157 Dumbest Criminal Stories (Kindle)

* Professor Birdsong's Weird Criminal Law Stories (Kindle)

* Professor Birdsong's "365" Weird Criminal Law Stories for Every Day of the Year (Kindle)

* Professor Birdsong's Weird Criminal Law Stories, Volume 2: Stories From Around the States and Abroad (Kindle)

* Professor Birdsong's Weird Criminal Law Stories, Volume 3: Stories from New York City and the East Coast. (Kindle)

* Professor Birdsong's Weird Criminal Law Stories - Volume 4: Stories from the Midwest (Kindle)

* Professor Birdsong's Weird Criminal Law Stories, Volume 5: Stories from Way Out West (Kindle)

* Professor Birdsong's Weird Criminal Law Stories - Volume 6: Women in Trouble (Kindle)

* Professor Birdsong's Weird Criminal Law - Volume 6: Women in Trouble! (Paperback)

* Immigration: Obama must act now! (Kindle)